A CHILD LIKE MINE

DEMORIS B. HICKMAN

COPYRIGHT

© 2021 by Demoris B. Hickman

All rights reserved. No part of this book may be reproduced or used in any manner without written permission of the copyright owner except for the use of quotations in a book review. For more information, contact:
morris30.motivated@gmail.com

All scriptural text is taken from the New Living Translation

Library of Congress Number: TXu 2-270-423

ACKNOWLEDGEMENTS

EDITOR: Dena Renee Crews is the editor for this work. While she has previous experience in journalism, this is her first time working in the fiction arena.

PUBLISHER: Kingdom Publishing, Inc. Stacey Mullins, Consultant

TABLE OF CONTENTS

PROLOGUE	7
THE PAST	8
CH. 1	9
CH. 2	12
CH. 3	17
CH. 4	28
CH. 5	32
CH. 6	37
CH. 7	45
CH. 8	58
CH. 9	72
CH. 10	84
CH. 11	89
CH. 12	102
CH. 13	105
CH. 14	117
AUTHOR'S MESSAGE	129

PROLOGUE

² Jesus called a little child to him and put the child among them. ³ Then he said, "I tell you the truth, unless you turn from your sins and become like little children, you will never get into the Kingdom of Heaven. ⁴ So anyone who becomes as humble as this little child is the greatest in the Kingdom of Heaven.

⁵ "And anyone who welcomes a little child like this on my behalf[a] is welcoming me.

Matthew 18:2 - 5 NLT

The Past

Rain clouds filled the sky as the minister spoke over the coffin. The young mother held her daughter close to her, barely listening to the preacher.
"We commit Abel Cartwright to these grounds, Lord, but we know this is not his final resting place. Ashes to ashes, dust to dust. We have hope to be resurrected into eternal life based on the promise of our Lord Jesus Christ. Therefore, we faithfully give Abel over to your blessed care, Lord. Amen."

The pastor walked over to the mother and shook her hand. She looked up at him, lost. *How in the world am I supposed to go on*, she thought? *Where was God when I needed him most? My husband is gone and it's just me and my daughter, what am I supposed to do?* She looked down at her daughter. *Will she even remember him?*

CHAPTER 1

Daughter and work - the two most essential things in Heather Cartwright's life. The 39-year-old single mother works at Calvary Elementary School in Charlotte, North Carolina.

Heather is not a single mother by choice. Her husband had a heart condition and died on an operating table. She used her energy for her students at school and her daughter, Katelyn, instead of grieving over her loss.

The memory of the moment that morning made her laugh as she walked down the hall of CES.

"Mom, you have lipstick coming out of the side of your mouth," Katelyn said with her face frowned up.

Heather looked in the rearview mirror, "Oh gosh, I can't go in looking like this." Heather dug for a tissue in her dash and began wiping.

"No mom, you can't. You look like a vampire thirsty for blood" Katelyn added giggling.

"Yes, I vant to suck your blood. I'm very thirsty for your blood," Heather said as she reached over to Katelyn, acting like a vampire.

"Mooom!" Katelyn exclaimed laughing.

A student snapped Heather out of her memory. "Hey, Mrs. Cartwright, me and my dad going to take our dogs out to the mountains we are going to hunt. You wanna go?"

"Oh, wow, that sounds interesting. I'm pretty sure your dad just wants you not me. It will be a great time for you to spend some time with your dad."

"Aww come on Mrs. Cartwright, please. I asked the last time and you told me you will think about coming," the boy persisted. Heather responded with a smirk, "I'm still thinking."

The end of the day came and Heather was still working in her classroom. *Just one more thing* she thought, *and then I'll be ready to go.*

"Mom, it's been 30 minutes. Can we go now?" Katelyn said, eager to go home.

"Oh, I'm sorry - just trying to finish up some things," Heather said as she continued to type. "Ok, done - let's go."

Chapter 2

Sometimes the memories were overwhelming. Heather looked at the pictures of her late husband and their daughter. Such happy times. Heather tried not to question God wondering *why*. She tried not to let bitterness creep in but focus on how God provided for her and Katelyn since that tragedy.

"Mom, what's wrong?"

Heather didn't realize that Katelyn had walked into the room while she was lost in her thoughts. "Nothing is wrong, just my allergies acting up again," she said, wiping away tears. "Hey, I need you to get ready for bed. Make sure you have your practice clothes packed in your bag for tomorrow afternoon."

"Yes, mom. Just don't be late picking me up. When you're late, Ms. Clark talks and talks and talks. She talks about the cheerleading squad and how it can be better if the school would just - blah blah blah."

Heather kissed the top of Katelyn's head, "I won't be late. So don't worry, Ms. Clark will have to share her concerns with someone else."

Later that night, Heather sat by Katelyn's bedside and they read the Bible together. Saying their prayers, Heather was again remaining thankful for God's provision and that she had her beautiful child with her.

The whistle blew in the gym.

"Hey, hey guys stop horsing around before you injure yourselves," one of the coaches said.

"Katelyn, can you come over for dinner tonight?

"I'll have to ask my mom. You know she's kinda overprotective of me when it comes to going places."

"I'll ask my mom if your mom can come too. My dad has to work tonight. It will be fun; besides, you need to eat anyways and gain some weight," she said with a smile.

"Whatever," Katelyn said as they walked out.

"So, Mrs. Cartwright, are you from here in Charlotte?" Mrs. Bowman asked as she served dinner.

Katelyn had begged Heather to go to her friend's house for dinner and she relented. "Yes, born and raised here."

"Me too; my husband is the outcast here though, - he's from Nashville," she said with a smile. "He decided to stay here after we got married. We love the city. Everything is convenient, especially the school. Marcia tells me how nice you are. How long have you been at the school?"

"It's been five years. I was going to stop teaching for a while after my husband passed, but I love the kids and they love me, so here I am."

"I am so sorry to hear that," Mrs. Bowman said.

"Thanks, we're ok," Heather said with a look of sadness.

"If you ever need anything, or if we can do anything for you, please don't hesitate to call me," Mrs. Bowman said.

"Will do, thank you."

"Do you have a church home? If not, maybe you and Katelyn can come with us some time," Mrs. Bowman inquired.

Heather looked down at her uneaten food. These conversations always made her uncomfortable. "It's been hard for me to go back since my husband passed. I still read my Bible and pray, but it's a struggle for me right now."

"I can only imagine how you feel. But know that God loves you and he has something special for you. Whenever you are ready," Mrs. Bowman said.

As they drove home, Heather thought about what Mrs. Bowman said. *How can I trust God completely after he allowed my husband to die? Yes, I love him, but my faith is just not where it should be. Yes, I still pray, but being back around other people praising God and listening to a preacher about his faithfulness...I just don't know. Do I believe in God? Yes. Do I trust him with my life? No, not after losing my Abel. But I have to think about Katelyn. Is this fair to her, letting my lack of faith keeping her from learning about God?* Heather sighed heavily to herself.

The rain poured down as Heather drove herself and Katelyn to Carver. "Mom, slow down. We'll get there," Katelyn said.

Heather sobbed most of the night and overslept. "I'm sorry sweetie. I didn't sleep well and don't want us getting there too late."

"Maybe you should take the day. I can catch a ride home."

"I'll be fine. Besides, they are having a hard time getting substitutes and I don't want just anybody with my kids. Listen, how would you feel about going to church with Marcia and her mom Sunday?"

"Oh, mom, really! That would be great."

"Yes, we've been gone for so long. It will be good to be back in service again."

Katelyn did a fist pump, yes. Heather looked at her daughter and smiled, then looking ahead, she drove through the light that just turned green as a car continued to go through the light that just turned red, hitting the passenger side…" Mooommmm"

"Kate……"

CHAPTER 3

Principal Shannon Hicks called and left a message for Heather, "take all the time you need, Heather. If you can't finish out the school year I understand. Just let me know."

The machine clicked off and Heather hugged the blanket closer to her body as tears continued to stream down her face. Katelyn was killed in the car accident. The driver charged with reckless manslaughter offered no comfort. The visits from family, friends and coworkers offered no comfort. Her mother tried to stay with her, but Heather sent her home, telling her she would be fine. Darkness enveloped her and she saw no light of hope. Mrs. Bowman visited often and tried to pray with her, but Heather only half listened and said *amen* to appease her.

I need to get back to work. I need something to do. This house is so empty. No husband, no child, no reason really to go on. I'm so alone.

Heather returned to work after a few weeks. Principal Hicks welcomed her back. "It is so good to see you. We have missed you. If there is anything you need, please let me know."

"Thank you, hopefully, I will be able to get back into the swing of things quickly," Heather said.

"There is a new student that is in your class. She transferred in last week. Sweet child, her name is Claudia. She is not afraid to speak … at all," Principal Hicks said with a smile.

"I look forward to meeting her."

Principal Hicks was quite accurate, Claudia was not afraid to speak at all. Heather found the nine-year-old to be full of joy and energy.

"Good morning, everyone. I am glad to be back with you. Let's begin the day with share outs. Who wants to go first?" Jeffrey eagerly raised his hand. "Alright, Jeff - share out."

"Ok, so yesterday I was playing with my pet frog. His name is Porky. I was having fun and then my mom got upset with me cause it hopped in her room and then she screamed." The class laughed uncontrollably.

"Ok, everyone calm down. Well, Jeff next time keep Porky in your room. Ok, who's next?

"Me of course," a small child with pigtails raised her hand.

"Yeah, let's hear what new here has to say," a student called out.

"Now, we won't have that. You must be Claudia. It is good to have you here with us. Share out."

Claudia stood up and walked to the front of the room. "My evening was with my parents at the church and oh Mrs. Green. I think she doesn't like me. She always giving me that funny look as if I'm not supposed to exist. *What kind of spirit is that in the church?* Church is supposed to be about love and having fun with family, me and my parents always have fun together!" Claudia spoke confidently.

"I go to one of those churches," a classmate called out and the other students laughed.

"Class!" The students' laughter died down. "I think it's great that you have fun with your parents. Keep it up."

"Yes, we do, Mrs. Cartwright and I can't wait until summer break when we go to the mountains. It's going to be great. I can't wait."

"I bet you can't" Heather said with a smile.

The day went by fast Heather stayed focused on her students and teaching; she didn't let her mind drift to her sorrows.

The principal called for students to be dismissed; as the classroom emptied, she noticed Claudia sitting at her desk writing in a notebook.

"Sweetie, it's time to go home."

"I know. I'm just writing down what I want to do for my family this month."

"That's sweet. What do you plan to do?" Heather asked as she sat next to her.

"Well, I really don't like to share until it's time to do it unless you promise you won't tell."

Heather crossed her heart, "Promise."

"I plan on raising money for my parents so we can have enough for our summer savings for our trip to the mountains. I heard my parents arguing last night because we don't have enough in our savings."

"I'm sorry to hear that."

"It's ok. I have a good plan, "Claudia said with excitement. "I want to have a bake sale here at school."

"We would have to talk Principal Hicks about that first to see if it's possible for you to have it."

"Will you talk to her for me?" Claudia said, hugging Heather.

"Sure. I will ask, but I can't make any promises. Ok?'

"You're the best teacher ever," Claudia squealed, hugging her tighter.

"Claudia," Heather turned to see a young African American woman standing in the door.

"Mommy," Claudia ran to the door.

"Hi, I'm Mrs. Cartwright, Claudia's teacher," Heather reached out her hand to Claudia's mother.

"Hi it's so nice to meet you," Claudia's mother said.

"It's good to meet you as well. I've enjoyed meeting Claudia; she is a very outspoken young lady."

"Mommy, I told the class about having fun and that old Ms. Green at the church…"

Her mom shook her head, "Never mind her, she's a bit much at times. We'd better get going. Her dad is waiting for us outside."

Claudia grabbed her book bag and notebook. She went to Heather and hugged her, "Don't tell, remember," she whispered.

"I won't," Heather whispered back, "See you in the morning."

The rest of the week went by fast. Heather was only alone in her thoughts, thinking of her husband and daughter at home. Saturday morning, she went for a jog around the new health facility that opened. Jogging took her mind off things, run it all away.

She stopped and looked at her watch to check her laps and sat on a nearby bench. A guy approached her, "Great day, isn't it?"

"Yes, it is," Heather said, hoping he would continue his run.

"You come out here often? This is my first time out here. I'm new in the area."

"No, not really. Only when I have some time," Heather replied.

"Oh, I'm sorry. My name is Henry, by the way - and you?"

"Heather," she said. They shook hands.

"Heather, it's nice to meet you."

"Nice to meet you too," she said with slight nervousness.

"Would you like a bottle of water? I have some in my cooler."

"No, thank you. I need to get home, got papers to grade," Heather said nervously, standing up.

"Oh, you're a teacher. Cool. Well, I hope to see you here again."

"Yes, that would be nice," Heather said and started to walk off.

"Hey," Henry said holding up a water bottle," you may need this."

Heather laughed, "Thanks, I better get going now."

"See you around Heather."

"See you around Henry," Heather said with a smile as she walked to her car. As she drove off, Henry was watching her; she smiled and waved.

"Lizzy, how many times do I have to tell ya there's no way we going to be able to make this trip this summer," Claudia's dad said to her mom as she listened through the closed door.

"Jack, we have enough money. I checked the account and we have it. Besides, you know how much this means to Claudia," Lizzy pleaded.

Jack spoke firmly, "We don't. That extra money is for the mortgage. I'm not getting any more hours to have extra to set aside so that money is to help keep a roof over our heads."

"Jack, just check it again."

"Check what - the account. No Lizzy. I'm done with this. We're not going this year and that's that," Jack walked towards the closed door and Claudia ran to her room.

Claudia heard footsteps and saw her door open. "Angel, why are you still up?" Lizzy said and sat next to Claudia on her bed while she pretended to read a book.

"Just reading before I go to sleep. Mom, are we still going to be able to go on vacation?"

Lizzy hugged her close, "that's the plan, sweetie."

"Can Mrs. Cartwright come with us?"

"No, sweetie. It's just for family. She's just your teacher and I know you enjoy her ... you've been talking about her nonstop all week." Lizzy was glad that Claudia was enjoying her new school and her teacher was willing to help her after school with her math work.

"Please, mom, can she come!"

"Not this time. And sweetie, I don't want you discussing our family business with her - ok?"

"But, mom..."

"No, but's. What happens in this house...stays in this house - do you understand me?"

Claudia held her head down, "okay."

Lizzy kissed the top of her forehead, "Now, get some sleep. Love you."

"Love you too, mom, good night."

"Good night, my angel."

Lizzy closed the door as Claudia pulled the covers over her head, disappointed. As Claudia went to sleep, Lizzy leaned against her bedroom door wondering about the trip.

The choir was singing and the church was packed. Claudia always imagined she was singing on the choir and her parents sitting in the pews watching her. Ms. Green passed by, giving a look that gave Claudia the creeps.

"Mom, why does Ms. Green look at me so upset or something?"

"Sweetie, I don't think she is looking mean; she's just old and set in her ways that's all. Ms. Green's been coming to the church since it first opened. She's really the only one still here since the church got started."

Claudia peeked over her shoulder, looked at Mrs. Green and turned away quickly when Mrs. Green looked her way. Claudia tried to focus on the choir and her dreams of one day singing with them.

Chapter 4

Claudia spent a lot of time with Heather after school getting help with math. Heather was enjoying her time with her. Claudia reminded her a lot of Katelyn. Spending time with Claudia took her mind off her life. Heather felt a special closeness with Claudia and was thankful her parents let her spend extra time with her.

Claudia's parents were concerned about the closeness. But Claudia was starting to excel in math and she enjoyed spending time with her teacher.

Lizzy opened the door to find Heather standing there. "Oh, Mrs. Cartwright, I forgot you were coming for Claudia. She has a ton of chores to do."

"Oh, it's fine. Another time then."

"No, mom," Claudia said, running to the door. "I promise I'll get all my work done. You said I could go."

Lizzy looked down at her daughter. "Mrs. Cartwright, how early can you have her back?"

"You give me the time, and that's when I'll bring her back."

"Two."

"Two it is. I'll call and let you know when we are on the way back." Claudia grabbed Heather's hand and took her away from the door, "Bye mom."

Heather took Claudia downtown to Discovery Place. They walked through looking and talking about the exhibits. When Heather dropped Claudia off, Claudia asked, "Mrs. Cartwright do you have a family?"

"I had a husband and daughter. They passed away."

Claudia reached over and hugged Heather. "It's ok, sweetie. I miss them, but they are in a better place now. You know you remind me of my daughter. Her name was Katelyn."

"I do. What was she like? Was she funny and smart like me?" Claudia asked, posing in her seat.

"Yes, as a matter of fact, she was," Heather laughed. "Come on, let me get you inside, so you can do your chores."

As they walked to the front door, Claudia asked, "Will you come to church with us tomorrow?"

"Maybe next time," Heather said uncomfortably.

"Aww come on, Mrs. Cartwright. You'll love the songs we sing. I be clapping my hands and praying with my mom and dad. I love church," Claudia said with excitement.

"I'm glad you do."

Lizzy opened the door before Heather could ring the bell. "Hey, how was it?"

"The Discovery Place was great. I have the best teacher in the world."

Heather chuckled, "I don't know about the best, pretty good but not necessarily the best."

"Mom, Mrs. Cartwright said she would come to church with us tomorrow…"

"I said maybe…." Heather interrupted.

"Oh, that would be great," Lizzy said.

Jack came from behind Lizzy, "Hey Mrs. Cartwright. Thank you for taking Claudia on the trip. Come on Claudia, you have some chores to get done. Have a good afternoon, Mrs. Cartwright." Jack closed the door.

On the other side of the closed door, Lizzy said, "Claudia, you can't just throw church on people and try to make them do something they don't want to do."

"But mom, she'll like it. You like it, dad likes it," Claudia begged.

"That doesn't mean someone else will like it. Ok?" Jack said.

"Ok," Claudia said sadly as she turned on the water to start washing dishes.

Chapter 5

The annual spring festival created a crowd in downtown Charlotte. People were everywhere.

"Hey there, you?" Henry said as he snuck up behind Heather.

"Oh, Henry, hi. You scared me. How are you?" Heather asked with a smile.

"Sorry about that. I saw you from a distance and thought I would come over and say hello."

"That was nice of you."

Henry continued, "I see you are out enjoying this great evening."

"Actually, this wasn't my idea. I'm here with one of my students."

"I remembered you were a teacher. Where's your student?"

Heather turned, "She's in the kiddie area playing with some of her classmates."

"That's nice of you, spending a Friday evening with one of your students."

"Her parents had to work and Claudia really wanted to go, so I volunteered."

As she finished, Claudia ran up, holding a small, brown bear. "Look at what I won Mrs. Cartwright. It has candy inside," she said opening up a piece.

"That's great. Slow down on eating all that candy, you'll cause yourself a stomach ache."

Claudia looked up, noticing Henry. "Who's this Mrs. Cartwright?"

"This is Mr. Henry. He likes to run. I met him at the track last week."

Claudia looked at Heather skeptically, "You run?"

Heather laughed, "Yes, Claudia sometimes I run."

"I'd like to see that," Claudia said popping another piece of candy in her mouth.

Henry smiled and spoke, "How about we go over to the fitness center and have a nice picnic? I can pick up some sandwiches and drinks if you like."

Claudia squealed, "Oh, can we? That sounds like fun."

"Maybe next time Claudia. Your parents will be looking for you shortly."

Henry replied, "Maybe another time."

"Sure. Have a good evening, it's time for me to get her home," Heather said, taking Claudia's hand.

"I hope to see you at the track soon. It was nice meeting you and I hope to see you again," Henry said to Claudia.

"Bye, Mr. Henry."

Heather was lost in thought as they walked to the car but she heard Claudia say, "He's nice, good looking too."

The church was packed as usual. Claudia noticed Ms. Green behind her; she could feel her watching her. She turned around and they locked eyes. Claudia turned around quickly, staring straight ahead.

After service was over one of Claudia's older cousins greeted them, "Hey family!"

They exchanged greetings.

"So, you guys getting ready for our big trip this summer?" Bubba said.

Claudia's parents exchanged looks. "That's the plan," Jack responded.

"Man, great. Keep us posted. We got our money set aside and we are ready to ride."

Claudia stood listening to the grown-ups talking and was lost in thought, knowing that her family may not make the trip. She was still hoping that the bake sale she wanted to do would happen and they would have the money to go.

"Little Angel how you doin?" Bubba asked snapping Claudia out of her thoughts.

"I'm good," Claudia answered.

"Sidney's always asking about you. She's with her grandparents this Sunday. You know what - she's having a sleep over next week - you should come."

Lizzy said "That would be great for Claudia. It will give her some time to spend with her cousin. She's been spending a lot of time with her teacher…"

"Her teacher…what's wrong, she need help or something?"

Jack responded, "She was getting some math tutoring, but Claudia really likes her teacher and just wants to hang out with her."

Bubba shook his head, "Oh wow. Wouldn't catch me hanging out with my teachers. I didn't even like school, I just liked lunch and recess."

They all laughed and continued to talk. Claudia thought of her plan, *I've got to raise this money for our trip. Time is ticking.*

him. But my momma doesn't want me sending a lot of time with him cause he drinks a lot."

"John, that's great that you want to spend time with your uncle. I think your mom just wants to make sure that you are safe."

Candace raised her hand, "I wish I could sleep at night."

The class started laughing. "Quiet!" Heather said sternly, "Let Candace talk and be respectful."

"My mom and dad argue a lot, I can't sleep. I just want to run away," Candace said clearly upset.

Heather walked over to her. "Hey sweetie, I'm sorry to hear that. Sometimes moms and dads have disagreements but that doesn't mean they love you any less. So don't run away," she said hugging her.

Claudia listened, thinking about her parents and their arguments wishing they would stop. She'd rather live with her aunt. Her house was quiet and she was fun to be with.

"Alright class, this is your journal topic for today. So, I want you to write about the one thing that would make you happy and why it would make you happy. You have ten minutes to get your thoughts down." As Heather spoke, she looked over at Candace and hoped that things weren't as bad as she said.

The church's board meeting was taking place at the same time Claudia was thinking about her parents. Lizzy's mind was somewhere else too. She wondered why her daughter enjoyed spending so much time with her teacher. *Am I not enough?* She wondered. Her thoughts came to an end when she heard several Amens. Goodness, the meeting is over. As she gathered her belongings, she caught the eye of Ms. Green.

"How are you feeling, Ms. Green?" Lizzy asked.

"I'm fine, why?" Ms. Green stared at her harshly.

I see why Claudia is intimidated by her. "After your fall at church Sunday, "Lizzy stammered, "just wanted to know if you were ok."

"Honey, I'm fine. There's nothing wrong with me," Ms. Green said and walked off.

"My Lord," Lizzy said staring after her.

Later that night at dinner, Claudia's father was talking. "Your cousin is coming over this weekend."

Claudia looked at her food and just twirled the spaghetti with her fork.

"Claudia, your daddy is talking to you. Stop playing with your food," Lizzy said.

"Sorry daddy," Claudia said continuing to twirl her spaghetti.

"You guys can help your mom organize some pictures for me that I'm bringing home."

"What kind of pictures?" Claudia said looking up.

"A friend of mine has some unique pieces that I purchased. I think they'll look really good in the living room."

Lizzy wiped her mouth, "That would be great to have Claudia home instead of running off with her teacher Saturday. It will be great to have you home to help out more."

"Please not tonight, Lizzy," Jack said leaning back in his chair and sighing.

"What do you mean, not tonight. We are her parents, not Mrs. Cartwright. She should be with us every Saturday, with her family - not with her teacher running around town like we can't take our child places," Lizzy said firmly.

"But mommy I like her and she likes me," Claudia left the room with tears streaming down her face.

"Happy now? Why did you have to say all that?" Jack asked.

"I am her mother. I don't want her *hanging* out with Mrs. Cartwright anymore."

Jack pushed back his chair and stood up, "I'm going to check on her."

Lizzy sat silently at the kitchen table. She knew she worked a lot but Claudia was her daughter. She felt she was losing her. She was fine at first with Heather helping Claudia and then offering to take her places but it was starting to be every Saturday. Lizzy felt she was only seeing her daughter at night when she got home from work. She was tired too and had to get food on the table. Something had to change. Lizzy shook her head and started to clear the table.

Jack opened Claudia's bedroom door. "Sweetie, you alright?" Jack walked in to find his only child on the bed crying softly. "Sweetheart, it's going to be ok. Your mom is just a little stressed, that's all," he said holding her in his arms.

"But, daddy, I like Mrs. Cartwright. She likes to go to different places. We do things different than me and mommy - we don't do that much," she said crying softly.

"Well, you know we work really hard to try and keep the bills paid and make sure you have everything you need so it takes a lot of our time, that's all. Hey, how about you and I have a date? I'll take you for some ice cream Friday afternoon before your cousin comes."

Claudia looked up at her father, "sure daddy."

Jack kissed her on the forehead, "Good deal. Now get washed up, it will be time for bed soon."

As Jack walked out the room, Claudia asked, "Daddy, do you like my teacher?"

"Sure, she's alright. We trust her or we wouldn't let you go with her."

"How come mommy doesn't like her?'

Jack sighed, "I think your mom is just concerned about you and wants you home, spending more time with her. I don't think she doesn't like her; she just misses you."

"Daddy, can we invite her to come to church with us? I think she would really like it."

"We'll see. Now go get washed," he said closing the door.

Claudia sat on her bed shaking her head. She tried to believe Jack, but deep down she felt her mother disliked Mrs. Cartwright. Claudia thought back to their old home. *We were happy. Mommy spent time with me. We would go to the park and play on the swings. Since we came here, the only thing mommy does is work and when she's home she's working – cleaning or cooking. She doesn't have any time for me.* Claudia dried her eyes and got her bed clothes and went to the bathroom to wash up and change.

The fitness center was filled with bright sunlight Saturday morning. Heather and one of the teachers from school were jogging around the track.

"Heather, I think the bake sale is a great idea. My kids are so excited and are already planning what to do with the money."

"I was so glad that Ms. Shannon set up the plan for this to work. Claudia really wants to help her parents with this money."

"Do they know about it?" Heather shook her head no, "Well they are in for one big surprise."

The women stopped and stretched. Henry ran up to them. "Hey ladies, how's it going?"

Heather responded, "Hi Henry. We are good, how are you?"

"Good. Are you free for dinner tonight, you can bring Claudia and I can show off my grilling skills?"

Heather laughed, "She's with her family today. But that sounds good."

"Ok, the two of us then. Come by about 6."

"See you then," Heather said smiling as Henry ran off.

"Hmmm, nice. Who is Henry?"

"Just a friend. I met him a few weeks ago. He's a member of the fitness center."

"Uh huh. I see you have your hands full. Very nice looking, are you dating?

"Oh no. Just friends," Heather answered.

"He seems quite a catch. This may be your time, Heather. Don't pass it up."

"He is nice but, I have no intentions of going any further."

"Heather, as your friend, let me give you some unsolicited advice. Moving on and finding love again does not take away from the love you had for your husband. It's time to love again, be happy and enjoy life."

Heather nodded, "Thanks, I do appreciate it. Besides, a guy like that is hard to find." They left the fitness center laughing.

Claudia's cousin, Bubba brought Sidney with him when he visited that Saturday. Sidney and Claudia worked on organizing the pictures with Lizzy while

Bubba and Jack sat on the back porch talking and laughing. After the pictures were put up, Lizzy joined the men outside. Sidney and Claudia went to her room to talk and play.

"Last year we had so much fun on vacation. I can't wait to go again," Sidney said.

"Yeah, we did," Claudia responded with disappointment in her voice.

"Claudia what's wrong?"

"I hear mom and dad arguing about not having enough money for the family trip."

"Oh no, you all always go. It won't be the same without you."

"I have a plan though. I hope it will work," Claudia said, looking hopeful.

"Oh yeah, what is it?"

"We all need help. The help of the Lord in your life will help you to love and forgive. If there is any confusion, any doubt, go to him. He cares for you," the preacher said as a chorus of *amens* and *hallelujahs* rang out.

Claudia noticed that Ms. Green wasn't at church and wondered where she was.

"Time is running out people. Don't hold on to grudges. Forgive one another while there's still time. Ya'll not talking to me in here. You don't know when the day will come when you will not see that person again. Love them while they are here. Forgive them while there is still time."

Once service was over Lizzy walked Claudia outside while her father talked with another member.

"Lizzy," one of the deaconesses called to her. "Can you take the minutes at the board meeting tomorrow; Ms. Green won't be there?"

"Yes, I can. Is she ok?" Lizzy inquired.

"You remember she fell last week," Lizzy nodded, "Well her leg swelled up and the doctor has put her on bed rest."

"Oh, my goodness. She told me she was fine Monday night. We will keep her in our prayers. She's tough, I'm sure this won't keep her down for long," Lizzy said.

"Ma'am, that's the last box," the delivery man said as he put the last box in her room for the bake sale.

"Hey, Mrs. Cartwright, I have a special delivery," the school secretary said as she walked into the room holding a vase with flowers.

"Oh my," Heather said.

"Wow, you got a good one," the delivery man said as he walked out.

Heather placed the flowers on her desk and opened the card that was attached. *When I close my eyes, I only see you because I see you from my heart. I hope you enjoy the flowers. Henry.*

Heather sat back in her chair and smiled. She smelled the flowers and wondered if things were moving too fast. *Can I really do this – move on? Henry's nice and generous. I just don't know if I can open my heart up. I don't want to fall in love and then lose him. I couldn't stand to feel this hurt all over again.*

CHAPTER 8

"How was school," Lizzy asked Claudia. Claudia didn't respond, lost in her thoughts. "Claudia Jean I'm talking to you. What's wrong?"

"Sorry mom. School was ok today. Mommy can I ask you a question?"

"Of course, sweetie, what you want to know?" Lizzy said smiling down at her.

"Frankie's Fun Park is having an event for our school Saturday. Can I go with Mrs. Cartwright?"

Lizzy stiffened. "Not this time. I'm off Saturday. How about we do something together? We never get to spend any time together except in the evenings and at church? You're spending more time with her than me. We can go to the park and swing like we used to."

"How are my favorite girls?" Jack said coming in the back door.

"We're good," Lizzy said receiving Jack's kiss, "just getting dinner started."

Claudia sat in silence willing herself not to cry.
"How is my angel?" Jack asked kissing her on the forehead.

"Daddy, mommy won't let Mrs. Cartwright take me to Frankie's Fun Park Saturday. I don't understand why she won't let me go with her."

"Claudia Jean stop it. I already told you that you will not go with her. Don't try to get your father to change it. I said no and I mean that."

"That's not fair. Mrs. Cartwright takes me fun places; you only take me to church and we sit around the house and clean. I want to go with her. I don't want to be here anymore – we don't do anything anymore like we used to. And you and dad do nothing but argue about money - I'm sick of it," Claudia balled up her fists running out the room.

Lizzy yelled after her, "Come back here young lady. You won't be raising your voice in this house."

Jack put his hands on Lizzy's shoulder. "Honey."

"No, Jack. I am sick of this. I'm losing my child to that woman. It was fine in the beginning. She was helping Claudia with her math and taking her to a few places we couldn't take her too, but this is going too far," Lizzy faced Jack with fire in her eyes.

"Lizzy calm down."

"I will not. As a matter of fact, I'm off on Monday, I'm going up to that school and I'm having her changed to another class. All we hear about is her teacher, Mrs. Cartwright this and Mrs. Cartwright that. She is not her mother. I am. She is not getting my child." Lizzy slammed the pots around and Jack resigned himself to the living room, not wanting another fight.

"How long has it been since you've been to church?" the therapist asked Heather.

"I haven't been back since my husband passed. I was getting ready to go back with my daughter, but then the accident. She had been trying to get me to go - so many times she would ask. I wish that I had taken her" Heather fiddled with her hands and started to cry.

"Heather, you are going to need to forgive yourself and learn to trust God again. It seems he is reaching out to you. The little girl you've told me about, Claudia - you said she has been trying to get you to do the same thing. God is reaching out to you and he wants you there for a reason. But you will have to go to find out" the therapist said handing her some tissue.

"I haven't been spending as much time with her. I don't think her parents want me to anymore. But I've fallen in love with her. She reminds me so much of Katelyn at that age."

"Do the parents know about Katelyn?"

"No, I don't believe they do."

"You need to tell them and build a relationship with them. You need to let them know that the relationship you have with their daughter is based on school and faith - that Claudia is encouraging you to come to church just like your daughter used to. If they are a godly family, they should understand. You need to tell your story Heather, and not hide from it. I truly believe that God has more for you, but you have to be willing to receive it and just be open."

Heather sat lost in her thoughts, thinking about what the therapist said. *God wants me. Was Claudia, who is so much "a child like mine" in my life to get me to God?*

Early Saturday morning, Henry was working on Heather's car. "It should be good to go," he said slamming the hood down.

"Henry, I really appreciate it."

"It's no problem. Anything for you. What do you have planned for the rest of the day?"

"I was picking up Claudia to take her to Frankie's Fun Park. They are having a fundraiser for our school today?"

"Oh, ok. Can I join you guys, I'm not doing anything?"

Heather stammered, "Uhm, maybe another time. You've done a lot here with the car, you should get some rest." *There would be other teachers and students and families there, I don't want a lot of questions I can't answer or figure out.*

"You sure?" Henry asked looking confused.

"Yes, we'll talk later Henry, ok?"

"I guess we will," Henry turned to leave disappointed.

"Oh Henry, your wrench," Heather said handing it to him.

"It can stay right here," Henry said and walked off.

Henry started the car, confused and disappointed. Each time he felt he was starting to understand Heather, she put him off. *I can't figure out if she likes being with me or not.*

"Excuse me, where do you think you are going," Lizzy asked Claudia watching her put on her shoes by the front door.

"Today we go to Frankie's for the school fundraiser," Claudia answered.

"Claudia Jean, I told you no. Didn't you understand?"

"Mommy why are you doing this?" Claudia whined.

"I am your mother and I make the decisions here young lady. Take your shoes off and go back upstairs. We are going to do something together."

Claudia yelled, "Like what mom, clean the house. I want to go with my friend. Why are you trying to stop me?"

"Number 1 - she is a grown woman, not a child, so she is not your friend. Number 2 - I am your mother and you will do as I say," Lizzy said pointing at Claudia.

Claudia stared back with tears flowing, "It's not fair mom. It's just not fair," Claudia exclaimed going into the living room.

Jack came downstairs, "What in the world is going on down here?"

"Claudia thought she was leaving this house to go to Frankie's Fun Park after I told her no. She's not going anywhere with that woman…I am her mother, not her," Lizzy answered hotly.

"Not again, Lizzy," Jack said as the doorbell rang. He shook his head and opened the door to find Heather standing on the other side.

"Mrs. Cartwright?" Jack said surprised.

"Hi, Mr. Simpson. Is Claudia ready?" Heather asked smiling.

Lizzy came to the door "Ready for what? Why are you here Mrs. Cartwright?"

Taken back from the response, Heather stammered, "Claudia said you said it was ok for me to take her to the fundraiser at Frankie's Fun Park today. She told me you were extremely busy this week..." her voice trailed off.

"Really, well I'll deal with her on that later. Mrs. Cartwright, my daughter isn't going anywhere with you today or ever again. I would like to spend time with my child. So why don't you get one of your own and leave mine alone."

"Lizzy, stop it," Jack intervened, "Mrs. Cartwright I do apologize..."

"Mommy what's wrong with you, why are you doing this?" Claudia yelled out and ran upstairs.

Jack pushed Lizzy aside, "Mrs. Cartwright I do apologize. We have some family things going on right now. Please forgive us."

Heather stunned, tried to smile and hold back tears, "I understand Mr. Simpson. I apologize I should have reached out to your wife. You all have a good day." Heather turned and walked off tears flowing down her face. Jack closed the door and sighed deeply, shaking his head at his wife.

"What is wrong with you?" Jack asked Lizzy. The change taking place in his wife was unsettling. She was being irrational.

Lizzy shook her head and walked off. *He wouldn't understand.*

Heather dried her tears and fixed up her make up before going in to Frankie's Fun Park. She didn't quite understand what happened, *why don't you get one of your own.* Claudia's mother's words kept ringing in her head. She had to move past this hurt and go in and spend time with the students and parents in her class. *This was supposed to be a fun day - for everyone.*

"Mrs. Cartwright, have you seen Candace," Ms. Walters walked over to Heather as she walked in.

"No, I haven't, just got here myself."

"I think she's run away. She wasn't in her room this morning," Ms. Walters said sobbing. Heather hugged her. "Mrs. Cartwright, I've tried everything to make sure she is happy. I know me and my husband fuss, we trying to make it right, I'm just so tired."

"It's ok. We are going to find her."

"Do you have any idea where she might be?" Ms. Walters looked at her hopefully.

"I think I do," Heather said.

"Sweetie you ready to go to the park?" Lizzy was standing in Claudia's bedroom door.

"NO!" Claudia said as she kept her head turned from her mother. She kept replaying the events of that afternoon and couldn't believe what happened. *Why was mommy being so mean to Mrs. Cartwright. I know she hurt her feelings telling her to get a child. She doesn't have one anymore. I hate living here. I wish we hadn't moved. Mrs. Cartwright is so nice and has time for me. I wish I could live with her.*

Heather told Ms. Walters where she thought Candace went and they rode together.

When they arrived at the house, they knocked hard on the door.

"I'm coming," a voice from the other side of the door said, "knocking on my door like they crazy."

A lady opened the door, "Sylvia. I've been wondering when you would show up."

"Is Candace here?"

"Of course, she is," the lady yelled out, "Candace, come here."

Candace ran to the door and Ms. Walters pulled her into her arms. "Candace, you had me and your dad so worried. He's running around the neighborhood knocking on doors."

"I'm ok momma."

"Thank you Tamela," Ms. Walters said to her sister.

"That's what sisters are for. Come on in. You don't come around anymore. Candace told me about what is happening at home. If you need to talk to me…oh who is this?"

"This is my teacher, Mrs. Cartwright," Candace said. The ladies shook hands and exchanged pleasantries.

"I will call. Thank you for watching her."

Tamela looked down at Candace, "Are you better now? You have people who love you little one. No more running away - although it did get your mom over here," she winked at Candace.

Laughing, Candace said, "Yes ma'am."

Tamela looked at her sister and Ms. Walters looked back at her sister as they walked to the car, "I'll call."

Church service was packed. The spirit was high, clapping, singing and dancing. Claudia was clapping and thinking *one day I'm going to be up there. One day my family is going to be happy again and there won't be any more arguments. Everything will be alright.*

When the service was over, Claudia noticed Ms. Green was back, limping slightly and with a cane. They made eye contact and Claudia lifted her hand to wave at her. Ms. Green stared back and turned to walk off.

Claudia frowned and turned around and saw the choir director. She ran up to her. "Can I join the choir?"

The choir director laughed, "Sure princess. Of course, you can. Once you are a bit older you can join the adult choir."

"How come we can't have a children's choir? I can't wait that long."

The choir director laughed and Lizzy walked over.

"Lizzy you have one amazing child here. She's ready to join the choir."

"She can be a handful sometimes, I'm sorry," Lizzy apologized.

"No worries, I love her eagerness. She mentioned a children's choir and it has been years since we have had one. I think it's time we get one again."

"Really. Who would be the director, you have your hands full with the adult choir?"

"You're right about that. Believe it or not, Sister Green used to be over the children's choir. There was an accident and she didn't want to do it anymore. I think it was too much for her or something. She was really good with the children."

Lizzy asked, "What accident?"

"Ms. Green was taking one of the girl's home from choir practice, one she was very close to - well, it was raining and Ms. Green lost control and hit a tree. The girl died at the accident and Ms. Green barely survived."

"I had no idea," Lizzy said.

"Yeah, it was a sad time for all of us. Sister Green didn't lose her faith, but she didn't want to work with the children anymore - too many memories. But God is a restorer."

Claudia thought about Ms. Green after hearing the adults talking. *She must be so sad.*

The choir director continued talking, "but I think the idea of having a children's idea is great. I'll bring it up to the board at the next meeting."

"Thanks. See you at the meeting," Lizzy said and took Claudia's hand and left the church.

Chapter 9

Claudia wasn't in class Monday morning. Heather felt her mom was going to try and change her from her class. It was too late in the school year for that. Heather had already talked to Principal Hicks about it. She didn't know what she had done wrong but had to change her focus to the twenty-one faces looking at her.

As she began to teach, Claudia came in escorted by the principal who looked at her and nodded.

Heather smiled down at Claudia and she smiled back.

Later during recess, Claudia came over to Heather.

"I really wanted to go to Frankie's with you Mrs. Cartwright," Claudia said.

"I know sweetie. But we have to respect your parents' wishes.

"My mom isn't like you though. She doesn't spend any time with me other than chores and going to church."

"A time will come when she will have more time to spend with you. She is your mother and she wants to spend time with you when she can. Hopefully we will be able to spend time together soon."

Claudia took her finger and motioned for Heather to bend down, "I love you Mrs. Cartwright," she whispered.

"I love you too, Claudia," Heather whispered back.

"Mrs. Cartwright, I can't wait for you to come to church with me. I'm trying to join the choir. You remember that lady, Ms. Green, I told you about. She use to be over the children's choir. They're going to talk to her about doing it again. I hope she does so I can join. And the first Sunday we sing, I want you to come. You will, won't you?"

"We'll see. Why don't you go play? Recess is almost over."

Claudia ran off and came back," Mrs. Cartwright, when can we do the bake sale?"

"The last week of school. Principal Hicks has already approved it. That should give us enough time to prepare the cakes. You will have to ask your parents about coming over to bake the cakes, especially since this is a secret," Heather looked at her and smiled.

"I'll be praying for God to touch their hearts so I can go," Claudia said and ran off to her classmates.

Heather smiled as she watched Claudia run off, *such a precious child.*

Ms. Green couldn't believe what they were asking her to do. "I don't know about this," she said as they discussed the children's choir.

"I think it's a great idea. This young lady is inspired and can't wait to sing. We need to let the youth use their talents for God," the choir director said to Ms. Green.

"I just don't know if I ever want to do this again," Ms. Green answered.

"Sister Green, I know what you have been through. You are going to have to let the past go. God understands. It was an accident. Come on, Sister! This little girl wants to do something positive - what do you say?"

"Give me some time to think about it. It's been years and I'm still hurt over the loss of that child."

"Pray about it. God could be sending this child your way to help restore you. I truly believe you should give it a try," the director said.

Ms. Green sat in silence, thinking to herself.

Henry had been trying to reach Heather since he worked on her car. He rang her doorbell. Her car was in the yard, why wasn't she answering. He waited until he thought she was home from work. He rang it again, tapping his foot. He tried one more time before shaking his head and walking back to his truck.

He sat in his truck, hoping to see some sign that Heather was home. He didn't understand what he did wrong and he wanted to fix whatever it was.

The next school day was busy. The fire alarm went off and Heather escorted her class down the hall and outside to the playground. As they waited for the all clear the curriculum coach came over to her.

"Mrs. Cartwright, how are you doing?" Monica asked.

"Doing good."

"That is one amazing girl you have in your class, coming up with the idea for a bake sale."

"Yes, she is."

"She reminds me so much of Katelyn - energetic, always smiling and full of ideas." Heather didn't respond. "Oh Heather, I am so sorry. How thoughtless of me."

"No, no, no. It's ok. Claudia does remind me of Katelyn - a lot. It's been good having her in my class."

"She's a blessing - that is so good."

Principal Hicks gave the all clear for the classes to go back in the building. Heather pondered what she had just heard.

"Jack, I don't know if I want Ms. Green around Claudia. She is afraid of her."

"Lizzy, I think Claudia will be fine. Ms. Green has been through lot."

"I don't want Claudia around her, she can't be on the choir," Lizzy said adamantly.

Jack threw up his hands, "You don't want her around her teacher, you don't want her around Ms. Green so she can't be on the choir. Lizzy do you hear yourself. What's wrong with you? Let's talk to Ms. Green cause I'm tired of hearing about this. I don't want Claudia missing out on what she wants to do because she's supposedly scared."

Claudia creeped away from her parents' door and went back to her room. She jumped in the bed wondering why her parents had to argue all the time.

Henry was at Heather's house ringing the doorbell again. This time she answered the door.

"Henry," she said surprised.

"I've been trying to reach you, is everything ok?" Henry asked.

"I'm ok, Henry, just tired." Heather had been avoiding Henry. The incident with Claudia's parents still bothered her.

"You haven't answered my calls…why?"

"I have a lot going on. Work, other things to tend to Henry."

Henry sighed, "I understand, just have been concerned. Can I come in?"

"Sure," Heather opened the door further. She closed the door once he came in and they sat in the living room.

"What is it, Henry?" Heather asked.

"Well, I've just been concerned. You haven't been yourself since we last saw each other. Did I do something wrong?"

"Henry, I've been busy with work. Besides we are just friends…you have things going on in your life too, I'm sure."

Henry looked frustrated and disappointed. "Yes, we are but I miss spending time with you."

"I'm sorry Henry, but I'm not ready for a relationship right now. I've been through a lot and I just can't. I'm sorry."

"So that's it."

"What do you mean?"

"You can't let go of the past."

Heather felt anger rising up, "let go! I lost my entire family in a matter of years. Let go!" Heather stood up and let out a heavy breath, trying to control herself, "Why did you come here?"

Henry stood up and walked over to her, "I want to help Heather. I want to be in your life. I want to help you get through this, but you can't keep holding on to the past. You have to want to get through it too."

"You don't know a thing about me. You don't know what I've been through - losing my husband and then my daughter. You know what," Heather walked to the front door angrily, "I want you to leave." Heather opened the door, "I want you to get out of my house now...."

"But Heather," Henry protested.

"Get out!" Heather cried.

Henry walked out the open door and Heather slammed it shut, falling on the floor crying uncontrollably. *How can he expect me to just move on? He doesn't even know me.*

On the other side of the door Henry shook his head in disbelief, tempted to knock on the door and get back in the house. *I love her. She doesn't see it, I want to help her and be with her.*

The sun shone bright Sunday morning as Jack and his family walked into the church. He had been preparing himself for what would take place after the service - talking to Ms. Green. He didn't know what to expect and he had a hard time focusing on the service. He was worried about Lizzy and her hostility towards Claudia's teacher and Ms. Green. Something was going on with her, she wasn't acting like herself at all.

"Jack, let's go talk to her before she leaves," Lizzy snapped him out of his thoughts.

Jack walked up to Ms. Green as she went to her car, "Sister Green," he reached out to touch her shoulder. "Can we talk? My wife and I have some concerns and questions if you don't mind."

"I don't mind at all. Go right ahead," Ms. Green said.

Jack looked at Lizzy who nodded for him to go ahead, Claudia hid behind Lizzy. "It seems our daughter is very uncomfortable around you. She says you stare at her and it scares her. We just want to understand what's going on. She wants to be on the choir but we can't let her if she is not comfortable around you, that is if you are going to do it."

Ms. Green opened her car door and sat down. "I see. I have a story. I'm pretty sure you've heard about it since you've been here. I've been at this church a long time, was over the children's choir. I took on this bright young girl, just like your daughter, I loved her dearly. There was an accident," Ms. Green teared up, "It was raining, a pop-up thunderstorm. I should have waited a little while longer but I didn't and that baby died and I lived."

Lizzy handed Ms. Green some tissue and touched her hand.

"I couldn't do the children's choir anymore, not after that. When you all came here, I looked at your baby…she reminded me so much of that little angel that was lost. I guess I couldn't help myself, I didn't mean to scare you, baby, you just reminded me so much of her."

"Sister Green is there anything we can do. You still are so troubled by this?" Lizzy asked.

"Her mother blamed me and left the church. I've tried so many times to apologize, but she wouldn't hear from me. She's away now and I just trust God for his forgiveness, healing and comfort."

"We'll be praying that God will open that door," Jack said.

"Thank you. Thank you both. Little Claudia you don't have to be afraid of me. I'm old and harmless," she smiled as Claudia looked at her from behind her mother and smiled back.

"But, Sister Green, we also wanted to ask you about the children's choir. We know there was a meeting this past week. Will you consider doing it? Our Claudia really wants to sing," Jack asked.

Ms. Green looked at Claudia and reached out to her; Claudia walked over to her and held her hand. "Tell me, why do you want to sing?"

"I want to praise God. I love to sing," Claudia answered strongly.

"Well, then I think we need to get ourselves a children's choir so you can praise God. You two just make sure you pick her up on time from rehearsals," Ms. Green said winking at Jack and Lizzy.

"Yay," Claudia said and hugged Ms. Green.

"Thank God!" Jack said.

Lizzy looked at her husband, smiling, and took his hand, "Yes, thank God!

Chapter 10

Claudia had been bouncy all morning and during recess ran up to Heather.

"Mrs. Cartwright, guess what?" Claudia asked excitedly.

Heather couldn't help but smile, "What?"

"I will be on the children's choir once Ms. Green gets it started."

"That is great news…but isn't she the one you said was mean?"

"Yeah, but she's not anymore. My parents talked to her and she's just been through a lot. She said she likes me."

"I don't see how she could not."

"Mrs. Cartwright, you will come when I sing won't you?" Claudia begged.

"Oh, sweetie. One day, we'll see. And you need to make sure that it is fine with your parents."

"I'm working on it. How's Mr. Henry? He's nice and I like him. He calls me sweet names."

"I'm sure you do. He is ok." Heather lied knowing she hadn't spoken to Henry since their argument.

"Can he come too? I want him to come with you."

"We'll see, now go play. Stop using up your recess talking to me," Heather said smiling. Claudia ran off and Heather wondered how Henry was doing. She didn't want to admit it to herself, but she did miss him.

"We all have to love one another as the Bible commands. In Mark 12:30 - 31, *Jesus says, 'Love the Lord your God with all your heart and with all your soul and with all your mind and with all your strength. The second is this: 'Love your neighbor as yourself.' There is no commandment greater than these.'* Jesus wants us to love one another. He wants us to show love to our neighbors. Who is our neighbors? Not just the person next door, not just the person in the pew next to you. Your neighbor is the person you run into at the grocery store, your neighbor is anybody that you come in contact with. Love your neighbor.

And, Jesus wants us to forgive one another. You say the prayer, *"And forgive us our trespasses, as we forgive them that trespass against us…another version says, "And forgive us our debts, as we also have forgiven our debtors.* We say the prayer but do we do the prayer. Come on somebody. Forgiveness shows love.

There's not one perfect, no not one. People are going to make mistakes. Ya'll hear me. People are going to make mistakes; you have to forgive. You have to forgive because your father in heaven has forgiven you, come on and praise God with me."

The pastor preached as Claudia and her family listened. Ms. Green was sitting next to Claudia and her parents were holding hands on the other side of her.

The pastor was bringing his sermon to a close, "Listen ya'll we need one another. Let's continue to show love and forgive one another. Let's impact the lives of those around us, we need each other…"

As the pastor finished, the choir sang. Ms. Green leaned over to Claudia, "That's going to be you one day."

"I can't wait. When do we start?" Claudia asked eagerly.

"I'm talking to the board this week."

After church, Jack and his family walked Ms. Green to her car. "Thank you, Sister, for agreeing to work with the children again. This means so much to Claudia."

"This church needs some young spirit going again. I'm starting to feel it again. All thanks to this little angel," Ms. Green said smiling down at Claudia.

"Ms. Green you work out?" Claudia said peering into Ms. Green's back car window.

"Claudia Jean stop being nosy. Excuse her Sister," Lizzy started.

Ms. Green laughed, "Oh it's ok. The doctor said it would be good for me to do some walking to help this leg. I'm going to the fitness center to walk the track. You should come with me some time Lizzy."

"Maybe when my schedule clears up."

"Mommy, that's where Mrs. Cartwright would take me walking." Lizzy frowned up and sighed.

Ms. Green asked, "Who's Mrs. Cartwright?"

Jack offered the answer knowing how his wife was still feeling about Heather, "She is Claudia's teacher."

"Wow. You have a good relationship with your teacher. That is so important. You must love school?"

"I do, I love it a lot."

"Well, good for you. Keep up the good work. I will be in touch."

Ms. Green closed her door and started her car as Jack, Lizzy and Claudia crossed the parking lot to their car.

CHAPTER 11

Heather woke up the following weekend to the house phone ringing and the doorbell buzzing. *Mercy, can't I just lay here in peace.* She turned over to look at the caller i.d. It was Henry. He'd been calling every day since they argued. She just couldn't bring herself to talk to him. His words hurt. She grabbed her robe and went downstairs to see who was at her door. She looked through the peephole. *I don't believe it.*

Opening the door she exclaimed, "Mom, what are you doing here?"

"Last I checked you were still my daughter. I haven't heard from you in days. Why haven't you answered my calls?" Sadie asked coming in with a duffel bag.

"Mom, I've just been busy."

"Too busy for your mother. I wanted to make sure you were alright. Heather, I know you are still hurting over Katelyn but you can't shut the world out, especially your family. I love you," she said holding her arms out.

Heather fell into her mother's arms enjoying the comfort and familiarity. "I love you too, mom. I'm sorry."

"No need for sorries. I'm here for you. We are all we have left. We have to stay connected, ok," she held Heather's face in her hands. Heather nodded. Sadie picked up her duffel bag and started to go upstairs.

"How long are you staying?"

"The rest of the month. I have more things in the car, you can throw on some clothes and help me get them out later."

Heather laughed, feeling good that her mother was with her. She could take her mind off of Henry and Claudia.

Across town that afternoon Ms. Green stood in front of fifteen children with the choir director. The children were on one side of the church, while their parents sat on the other side.

"Ok, you will write your name on this paper if you want to join the choir. Sister Green will be the choir director and she will go over some procedures for you and your parents," the choir director said as he passed around a clip board.

"I am excited that so many of you are interested. We will rehearse every Saturday afternoon from 4 pm - 6 pm. Parents I need you to pick your children up right at 6 pm. You are more than welcome to stay for the rehearsals, but I will need for you stay in the back and not interrupt."

Ms. Green shared more procedures and when it was Claudia's turn to write her name on the paper, she looked over at her mom and smiled widely.

"So, how did things go today, my soon to be lead singer of the children's choir?" Jack teased as he cut into his meatloaf.

"It was good. We just signed up today and Ms. Green went over a bunch of rules and stuff."

"I'm so proud of you and can't wait to hear you sing with the choir," Jack said.

"Thanks daddy!"

Jack looked over at Lizzy who was eating quietly. "Sweetie you're not going to say anything. Aren't you happy about it?"

"Sure I am. I am proud of you Claudia. I just hate how this means more time away from me," Lizzy shook her head and stabbed her food with a fork.

"Seriously Lizzy. This again. Come on, For god's sake Lizzy."

"Yes, this again. It's not ok. I want time with my own child just me and her. First her teacher and now Ms. Green and the choir."

Claudia's eyes filled up with tears, "Mommy I can't never make you proud of me," she ran out the room. Jack threw down his napkin.

"Happy now Lizzy. See what you've done. This mess has got to stop," he said getting up from the table.

Heather kept having the same dream over and over. She and Katelyn laughing together in the car and then the accident. Heather woke up with a start. She sat up in the bed pondering over whether to try and go back to sleep. She put on her robe and went to the kitchen. She found the light on in the living room. Her mother was sitting on the sofa with a photo album opened in her lap.

"Mother you alright, why are you up?" Heather asked crossing over to her.

"Couldn't rest. Come sit," she said patting her hand on the sofa beside her.

"Look at you. You were so young and the most beautiful girl … your father and I wanted you to have everything including all the happiness in the world. You were all we had," she said smiling running her fingers across a picture of Heather as a child. Heather looked at the picture with her mom.

"There is nothing like the young days, you are all grown up now," Sadie said turning the pages in the book. "Your dad is gone and I wonder what he would say today looking at his little girl all grown up. He would be so proud of you." Heather grabbed her mom's free hand and squeezed it overwhelmed with emotion. Sadie stopped on a page with Heather as a child and a picture of Katelyn.

"Katelyn looked just like you as a child. I miss her so much."

Heather teared up, "I can't, I can't do this. I haven't gone through that photo album since the accident. She used to always like to look at the pictures."

"Honey it's your daughter, look at her," Sadie encouraged.

"You don't understand. I'm the one suffering. She lived with me; she was a part of me. I just can't," Heather said and walked out of the room in a hurry.

Sadie followed her, "Heather, come back. Heather," she called but Heather went up the stairs and closed her bedroom door sliding on the floor in a fit of tears.

Saturday morning, Heather left the house. She needed to get out. The night before was horrible and she needed some air. Sadie tried to talk to her, but Heather told her she needed some time to herself and was going for a walk at the fitness center.

Heather was having a hard time focusing on the road, the lack of sleep, the flashbacks of the accident and images of Katelyn and her husband kept flooding her mind. Cars were passing her and blowing their horn, she didn't realize she was weaving in and out of lanes. She sat up straighter and tried to focus, but drowsiness was overtaking her. Her head dropped and when she looked up, she heard a horn blaring at her and a truck coming at her. She quickly turned the wheel into the correct lane, but not letting up speed she overturned, hitting a fence. The last thing she remembered was seeing the airbag deploy before she passed out.

Saturday afternoon, all the children that wanted to join the choir were on time. Ms. Green lined the children in the choir stand and introduced them to the song. Claudia volunteered to lead and Ms. Green worked with her.

"Sweetie, I need you to a hit a high note on the end there so the audience can feel your voice," Ms. Green said to Claudia. "Ok, we are going to go through it again, I'll cue you to start." Ms. Green pressed play on the CD player and Claudia's voice echoed in the sanctuary.

The pastor was standing outside the sanctuary doors with a deacon. "Will you listen to that?"

"That baby can sing," the deacon said.

"That girl is a light. We have to keep her and the rest of the children in the church. We can't lose them to the world. That child is a blessing and having the children's choir back is the first step in keeping our children in the church."

The song ended, "Great job everyone. I am so proud of each of you. Be ready Sunday," Ms. Green smiled at Claudia and Claudia smiled back.

When choir practice was over, Lizzy was outside waiting for Claudia. Claudia ran to the car.

"Hi, Mommy."

"Hey there. How was practice?"

"It was good. I'm singing lead to a song. Ms. Green worked with me. Mommy she's nice."

"Yes, she is. We just didn't know her before," Lizzy drove silently. "Sweetie, I owe you an apology."

"Ma'am," Claudia looked at her mother wide eyed.

"I've been overreacting. I just want to spend time with you. Things have been hard since we moved here and work takes up my time. It seems when I am home, you've been with Mrs. Cartwright and now the choir. I just miss you."

"Can we start doing things together?" Claudia asked.

"I'm going to try my best to make it work - for me and you. OK?"

"OK. Mommy how come you don't like Mrs. Cartwright?"

Lizzy sighed, "It's not that I don't like her, it's her getting all the time with my daughter. She doesn't have children of her own? I mean she was spending a lot of time with you and you have a mom."

"Her daughter died in a car accident. That's why she wasn't at the school when I started."

Lizzy pulled in to their driveway. "Oh my God. Oh my God. I need to apologize to her. Oh my God. I had no idea," she turned and looked at Claudia. "She just wanted to spend time with a child like mine." Lizzy pulled Claudia close to her in a hug. "I'm going to call and apologize to her. I'm sorry Claudia, I just don't want to lose you."

"You won't mommy. I'm not going anywhere," Claudia smiled.

Lizzy laughed and got out the car reaching for her phone in her purse. Jack came outside, "Well I'm glad my girls are home."

Claudia ran to her father, "Daddy, mommy's going to call Mrs. Cartwright. Does this mean I can go places with her again?"

Lizzy looked for Heather's number in her phone, "How about we all try and do something together sometimes?"

"Yes!" Claudia said pumping her fists and running into the house.

"Hello, Mrs. Cartwright?" Lizzy spoke into the phone.

"This is her mother," Sadie responded.

"Oh, this is Claudia's mother. I just wanted to speak with her if she is free."

"Oh, Heather told me about you. She is in the hospital. She was in a car accident this morning."

"Oh, my goodness. Which hospital?

"Carolinas."

"I am so sorry; we will be praying for her. How is she doing?"

"Still unconscious but by the grace of God she will be alright."

"Thank you, we will come up."

"Thank you."

Lizzy hung up and walked into the house nervously. Jack looked at her when she walked in, "Lizzy what's wrong?" He said as he walked over to her.

"Mrs. Cartwright was in a car accident. She's at Carolinas."

"Who's at Carolinas?" Claudia asked walking into the hall.

Lizzy bent down to her, "Sweetie, Mrs. Cartwright was in a car accident this morning. I just spoke to her mother."

Claudia started to cry, "We have to go see about her?'

Jack said, "Let's go."

"Yes, let's see if there is anything she needs," Lizzy said.

Claudia and her parents walked into the hospital room to find Sadie and Henry sitting on each side of Heather's bed. Fluids were flowing through the IV and large bandage was on her hand and her wrist was wrapped.

Claudia walked over to the bed, "Mrs. Cartwright please be alright, please come back." Claudia cried and Lizzy hugged her close. "Mommy, why did this happen?"

"Shhh sweetie, she's going to be ok. She just needs to rest," Lizzy said feeling guilty for how she treated Heather.

The doctor came in and asked everyone to leave. Lizzy and Jack took Claudia home, promising to bring her back to visit.

"Thank you for coming," Sadie said going to the family room. Henry followed her, "Henry, Heather would appreciate your being here," Sadie said.

"I wouldn't be anywhere else," Henry said sitting across from Sadie.

"She's told me a lot of nice things about you."

"I'm glad. We haven't talked in a while. I've been calling - I just figured she needed some space and time. I wasn't planning to try and call today but I felt I needed to...and I'm glad I did."

"Hmmm…. Funny how the Lord works. You called and I had to tell you about the accident, that little girl's momma called. It's all for a reason," Sadie said as she sat back.

The doctor came out of Heather's room, "She's recovering well. We will keep her to run some tests. She hit her head pretty hard and there is a fractured bone in her wrist. But she will be fine."

"Thank you, doctor," Sadie said. She looked at Henry. "Henry, you don't have to stay."

"I want to. I want to be here when she wakes up."

"You're a good man, caring for my daughter. She will recognize the good in you."

Henry sat back in thought willing her words to be true. He'd never felt this way about any other woman and he wanted Heather to feel the same way about him too. The thought of losing her, hurt. He had to stay to make sure that she was alright and that she knew that he would always be there for her.

CHAPTER 12

Heather stayed in the hospital a few days before she was released. The doctor reminded her to take her medicine for the headaches that would come. Heather still couldn't believe what had happened. *I really need to continue my counseling sessions. They were helping.* Her memory felt fuzzy but she remembered Claudia and her parents being in the hospital and Henry. *Henry, how did he know. He came everyday like clockwork and just sat by her side holding her hand. Claudia's parents were there too. How did they know and they brought Claudia to see her...I thought they didn't want her around me? I'm so confused.*

The nurse came to the room with the wheelchair.

"Henry, will you wheel Heather out while I get the car," Sadie said.

"Yes, ma'am."

Sadie walked out and Henry and the nurse helped Heather into the wheelchair.

"Henry, I'm sorry I didn't return your calls. I've just been stressed. I've been through so much. Please forgive me."

Henry stopped the wheelchair and walked in front of it and kneeled down in front of Heather.

"Heather, I do understand. I'm here for you. I'm just glad that you are going to be ok."

"Henry, one more thing. I'm ready to go back to church. If the offer still stands, I would like for us to go together."

"Definitely. It's time for both of us," Henry said as he went back to pushing the wheelchair.

Outside of the hospital, Claudia stood with her mother and father with a *Get Well Soon* balloon.

"Mrs. Cartwright," Claudia yelled running to her.

"Aww Claudia, thank you."

"Mrs. Cartwright we are glad that you are doing better," Jack said.

"Yes," Lizzy said. "We were all concerned and have been praying for you."

"Thank you," Heather said stunned.

"Well, we are going to let you go, so you can get home," Lizzy said.

"Thank you for coming and for letting Claudia come see me."

Lizzy touched Heather's hand, "No problem, Please forgive me for how I acted towards you. I am truly sorry."

"I forgive you," Heather said.

CHAPTER 13

Heather was back at work and it was time for the bake sale.

Principal Hicks was making an announcement for the bake sale, "This is our first end of the year bake sale. Prices for cakes, cookies, brownies and other treats are posted in the cafeteria. Cash only - no checks or credit cards," she laughed. "You will be able to make purchases during your lunch time only tomorrow. Have a good afternoon."

Claudia's parents let Heather take Claudia home with her that afternoon to bake and spend the night. They told them about the bake sale, but not what the money was going to be used for.

"Thank you, Mrs. Cartwright for helping me with the bake sale," Claudia said as she cracked eggs into a bowl. Sadie walked in.

"You are quite welcome."

"Smells good in here, can't wait to have a piece of one of these cakes tomorrow," Sadie said.

"I have something for you Claudia," Heather said as she dried her hands and went to her bedroom.

Sadie helped Claudia in the kitchen. "You are a special little girl with a good heart. God is favoring you princess. Your parents are blessed to have a wonderful daughter like you. Not matter what happens in life never give up your love to help others. Use that great talent God has given you to inspire others."

Heather went to a drawer in her bedroom and took out a small box. Inside was a necklace. She took out the heart necklace and held it in her hands with tears filling her eyes. It had been Katelyn's. She didn't bury her in it, she wanted to hold on to it. She had been wearing it on the day of the accident. Claudia reminded her so much of Katelyn that she wanted her to have it. It wasn't doing any good in a box, and she would rather see someone as good as Claudia to have it. She truly believed that Claudia was a gift from God. *Helping me to move on, to continue to live. Claudia has given me hope. I lost Katelyn and God sent Claudia in my life - a child like mine and the bond is inseparable.* Heather kissed the necklace, smiled to herself and went back downstairs.

"She's back," Sadie said.

"Mrs. Cartwright we only have one more to bake," Claudia said with excitement.

"That's great sweetie. I have something for you," Heather said, handing her the box, "open it."

Claudia opened the jewelry box and Sadie held her breath as Claudia took out the necklace.

"A necklace," Claudia squealed and hugged Heather around her waist.

"Mom will you put it on her, it's still hard for me to maneuver with my wrist like this."

"It would be my pleasure," Sadie said holding back tears. Sadie took the necklace from Claudia and fastened it around her neck. "This is a beautiful thing you've done Heather. She deserves it."

"It was my daughter, Katelyn's necklace. I want you to have it now Claudia," Heather said choking back tears.

"Aww thanks Mrs. Cartwright," Claudia said giving her another hug.

"So beautiful. You deserve it. Now let's get these cakes sliced and packed for tomorrow."

That night Lizzy and Jack were lying in bed talking.

"How are we going to tell her Jack?"

'I don't know. It's not going to be easy, but we need to let her know now that we won't be going on the family vacation this year."

"I just kept hoping that something would work out," Lizzy said.

"Yeah, well it didn't. We can't afford it this year."

"I don't think we need to say anything now."

"It's the last week of school. She'll be looking to go on the trip as soon as school is over. We can't wait," he turned over and turned off the bedside lamp. Lizzy lay on her back thinking about how this news was going to affect Claudia.

Henry packed the boxes of cakes in Sadie's car as Heather and Claudia settled in. "Well, you are all set, that's the last one," he said shutting the trunk.

"Thanks Henry, I really appreciate it," Heather said.

"Thanks Mr. Henry," Claudia said from the back seat.

"No problem little lady. Enjoy the bake sale, I hope you all sell out and make lots of money. I'm sure these are some good cakes," he said giving Claudia a thumbs up. Claudia gave him a thumbs up back.

"Are you stopping by? They are letting visitors in?" Heather asked.

"I'll try. I have some meetings at work, but I will try. I'll give you a call later," Henry said staring into Heather's eyes.

"Thanks again for everything Henry."

Sadie started the car, "Henry you are a good man. Thank you, the good you do is always needed - don't forget that."

"Thank you, ma'am," he said and waved as they drove off.

"We need to pick her up from school early and tell her. Maybe take her to get something to eat so it won't be so bad," Jack offered. Lizzy stared, stirring her coffee.

"Maybe we can try Frankie's. That way she can play and eat and maybe it won't bother her so much," Lizzy's voice trailed off.

"Yeah, let's do that. We'll pick her up around her lunch time."

Teachers and students were buying from the bake sale. Some teachers bought cookies for their entire class so everyone would have something from the bake sale. Claudia was smiling at how people were coming together. There were parents that came and bought items and one man from a local business bought a whole cake. Claudia couldn't stop smiling. *We're going to make enough money for this trip. Mommy and daddy will be so proud.*

Sadie looked at Claudia, "Looks like a success young lady."

One of the assistants came to Heather, "Mrs. Cartwright do you have everything you need?"

"Yes, we are good."

Principal Hicks came in and walked over to the table of baked goods. "Claudia this was a great idea you had. Your parents must be so proud of you?"

"They don't know," Heather said. "She plans on surprising them with the money for a family trip."

"Oh, that is so sweet. They are going to be surprised. I'm going to buy a few pieces of cake so I can be prepared for this meeting I have to sit through," she said smiling.

Principal Hicks went back to her office and Heather saw Henry make his way through the crowd.

"You made it," Heather said smiling.

"Mr. Henry, you came," Claudia said jumping up and down, running to him to give him a hug.

"Oh, you are such a bundle, little lady," Henry said hugging her back. "How is your bake sale going?"

"It's going good. I already sold over half of the cakes," she answered.

"Little lady you are such a blessing. Continue to do great things," he said.

"I will," Claudia answered proudly.

"Claudia, go see how many more cakes we have left," Heather said and Claudia ran to the area where the cakes were being kept. "

"So, how are you?" Henry asked Heather.

"Fine now. You know after the accident; I felt the Lord speaking to me about my life. I'm finally starting to feel me again," she said.

"Heather, I believe God spared your life from the accident. You're still here and he has some great things in store for you. In life we face difficulty and trials but we can overcome them if we don't lose our faith," he said.

"You're right. I guess at the time I was just going through so much and wanted to just forget about all that has happened. I can't do anything to bring them back."

"Your husband and daughter are in a better place. You have to live. God will bring people in your life to help you heal. He will bring you love, joy and peace. That little lady loves you and looks up to you," he said lowering his head and added softly, "I do too. You have an opportunity to speak into her life. You are a great woman, Heather."

"Thanks. She reminds me so much of my daughter. I love her," Heather said.

"I bet you do," Henry said as they smiled at each other.

"Mrs. Cartwright have you seen my daughter? We need to take her out early." Lizzy came up to the table.

"Hi," Heather said surprised. "Claudia will be surprised to see you. She just went to the back to see how many cakes we have left. I'll get her."

"You all have a special girl," Henry said reaching out his hand to Jack and Lizzy.

"Yes, we know she can be a handful," Jack said.

"Claudia your parents are here to pick you up." Heather found Claudia trying to hold several cakes.

"Why are they here? They never come this time of day to pick me up. I'm not ready to go, We aren't finished with the cake sale."

"Claudia, I think the only way you'll get to stay is if you tell them what the bake sale is for."

"I don't want to. It'll ruin everything."

"Come on, I will help explain," Heather said wrapping her arms around Claudia.

Heather and Claudia walked out the back holding more cakes and placed them on the table.

"Surprise, we are taking you out of school early so we can spend some time together," Lizzy said.

"But we are having the bake sale. I can't leave right now."

"I know sweetie, but I'm sure Mrs. Cartwright can handle it."

"But it's my bake sale," Claudia said.

Jack looked confused, "What do you mean, 'your' bake sale?"

Heather spoke up, "She was planning on surprising you both," she motioned for them to follow her."

Lizzy looked confused and irritated, "What do you mean a surprise for us?"

"She wanted to help out with your family trip this year. Claudia told us she overheard the two of you talking and said that you may not have the funds to go this year…so she wanted to help raise the money for you and surprise you with it," Heather explained.

Lizzy hugged Claudia close to her, "Aww sweetie. I'm so sorry. We didn't realize you heard us and were worried about the trip. As she hugged Claudia, she felt something. She looked at Claudia and noticed the necklace. "Where did you get that necklace from?"

"Mrs. Cartwright gave it to me," Claudia answered.

Lizzy felt herself start to burn. "Mrs. Cartwright, I appreciate everything you have done for Claudia, taking her places and helping her with her work - but this goes too far. Claudia is my child, not yours. You are not to give her anymore gifts. I will provide for my daughter. And Claudia, no more sharing our family business again with anyone…do you hear me?"

"Listen, she was just trying to help. I didn't mean any harm in giving her the necklace. She is such a special child…"

"You don't think I know that," Lizzy said hotly with her voice raising. She snatched the necklace off Claudia and handed it to Heather. Sadie and Henry looked over at them.

"I don't know. You are very busy…"

"Mind your business Mrs. Cartwright and stay out of our business, "Jack reached over to Lizzy and she shook him off. "Your services are no longer needed. As a matter of fact, Claudia won't be back for the rest of the school year. It's the last week anyway and I know ya'll ain't doing anything," she said and grabbed Claudia storming out of the cafeteria.

"I'm sorry Mrs. Cartwright," Jack said as he followed after them. Henry walked over to Heather and wrapped his arms around her, "It's going to be ok." Heather shook her head feeling unsure, looking at the broken necklace in her hand.

CHAPTER 14

Claudia couldn't believe what happened. *How did my plans get ruined so fast? Why does mommy hate Mrs. Cartwright so much? She's been so nice to me, taking me places and spending time with me. I don't understand.* Claudia put her face in her pillow and sobbed while her parents argued downstair.

"Lizzy you've got to get a grip on yourself. She was only trying to help."

"I don't care. What happens in this house, stays in this house. She should have come to us, not HER," she yelled.

"What is wrong with you?" Jack yelled back. "Tell me what is going on."

"I'm doing my best as her mother. I don't want her to feel the way I did growing up. My mother always working, never having time for me. I don't want her to resent me and want somebody else," Lizzy screamed.

Jack put his arms around her. "Lizzy why didn't you tell me? You are not going to lose Claudia. Things will get better for us."

Claudia couldn't take it anymore. She was tired of the arguing and her mom being mean to Mrs. Cartwright. She couldn't believe her mom broke the necklace and gave it back to her. *She wanted me to have that. It was her daughter's. Mrs. Cartwright looked so sad when she did that.* Claudia packed some clothes in her book bag and walked out the back door as her parents continued to argue. *I'm going to live with Mrs. Cartwright,* she thought to herself as she closed the door quietly.

The police were in the living room taking notes. Jack was pacing back and forth and Lizzy was on the sofa wiping tears.

"She must have left during night," Lizzy said.

The police officer asked, "Any reason why she might run away from home?"

Jack and Lizzy looked at each other. "We were arguing last night. She must have heard us," Jack said holding his head down. Lizzy's phone pinged and she got up to look at it.

"She's at Mrs. Cartwright's. She just sent a text. Claudia is with her," Lizzy said. "Thank God."

The police officer closed his note pad and rose, "I'm glad you found her. Keep an eye on your girl," he said and walked out.

Heather and Sadie tried to calm Claudia down. She showed up at the house early that morning crying and banging on the front door.

"It's just not right. I was only trying to help and they still argue."

"It's going to be ok Claudia," she said wrapping her arms around her.

"You all need to sit down and talk and get this squared away," Sadie said. "It's not fair to this child." Henry walked in with coffee and a juice for Claudia.

The doorbell rang and Sadie opened the door to find Lizzy and Jack.

"Where is she?" Lizzy said rushing past him. "Oh Claudia," she said going over to her and hugging her. "You scared us so bad. Don't ever do that again."

Jack went over to Heather, "Thank you for watching her."

"Would you all like some coffee," Henry offered.

"No thank you, we are taking our daughter home," Lizzy said.

"I don't want to go," Claudia said. "All you two do is argue. I was just trying to help and you broke Mrs. Cartwright's daughter's necklace."

Sadie put her arms around Claudia.

"I think we should have that coffee Henry is offering and sit down and talk," Sadie said.

"I agree," Jack said, "coffee sounds good."

Henry led the adults to the kitchen and left Claudia in the living room looking at television. As Henry filled more coffee mugs, Sadie talked. "We all need to come together for the sake of this child. She needs guidance not confusion. I was a little girl once and I had so many dreams but because of family matters, it was shattered. My father was an alcoholic and my mother left because of the abuse. I had to grow up faster than what I wanted. This child here, Claudia, she needs to be loved. She needs to see you all working together loving her, not being against each other. I advise you all to get it right - right now. Heather?"

Heather looked at her mother, "I only wanted to help your daughter become great. I care for her like my own daughter. She reminds me a lot of her, of my Katelyn. I am sorry if I offended you both in any kind of way. I only wanted to support your daughter in the best possible way."

Lizzy spoke next, "I was wrong. I was jealous. You were getting all of her time and with my work schedule I felt I was losing her and I took it out on you. I shouldn't have come at you like that. You have done a great job with Claudia. Please accept my apology."

Heather reached out to Lizzy and took her hand. "I do. We all have ups and downs. After my accident, God woke up my spirit. I was so lost after my daughter died that I forgot who I was. Your daughter brought hope back in to my life. Seeing that smile and warm spirit helps me. She has impacted my life."

"I am so sorry about your daughter and I was overreacting. I'm sorry about the necklace. I will pay to get it fixed so Claudia can have it. I just," Lizzy started and looked down. "Growing up my mother worked all the time. I never saw her. It was my grandmother that really raised me. I resented her. I saw my cousins with my aunts and would wonder, where's my mom. I just don't want Claudia to feel the same way about me. The more she talked about you and the places you took her to, the more jealous I would get. It wasn't fair to you or to her. I am so sorry."

Heather squeezed her hand, "I understand. I guess I should have told you both about Katelyn. I see so much of her in Claudia. They both love to talk," as she said this, they all laughed. "Both so inquisitive and loving. I guess part of me felt by keeping Claudia close, I was keeping Katelyn alive. But Claudia has helped me. She has opened my eyes to some important things missing in my life…God and love. I am so very grateful for her."

Sadie looked at them both as the men stood off looking at each other and drinking their coffee. "You two are finally getting the picture. Let love do its perfect work. God works all things for good. Claudia helped both of you realize what you were missing in your lives - love, grace, mercy and forgiveness. Ok, now a big ole family hug," Sadie said with her arms wide open.

As they hugged, the sun shone brightly through the kitchen window warming the room and their hearts.

Mrs. Green was at the church early. The children's choir would be singing that morning.

"Good Morning, Sister Green," one of the deaconesses said, "you're here early."

"Yes, the children's choir is singing this morning. I just want to make sure everything is in place."

"That's great. I am so glad that you are directing again. Your gift has been missed," the deaconess said and walked off. Mrs. Green smiled, thinking *God has prevailed once again, yes once again. Brand new mercies.*

Sunday morning, Lizzy, Jack and Claudia were at Heather's house for breakfast. They planned to meet there and go to church to hear Claudia sing.

Henry and Jack called everyone to the dining room, "Breakfast is served."

Sadie sat and looked at Jack and Henry, "Now where have you men been all my life?" She asked teasingly making everyone laugh.

"We have some good news. Tell them Lizzy," Jack said.

"I have a new job working from home. I got my realtor license. I'll be able to create and work my own schedule."

"Congratulations," Heather said. "That's great news. You and Claudia will be able to spend more time together.

"Well, everyone, hold on. There's one more announcement," Henry said.

"You got a new job too?" Claudia asked and the adults laughed.

"I hope to have one," Henry said as he kneeled down in front of Heather. "The best job in the world for me is if I can be your husband. Heather, will you marry me?" He opened up a ring box.

Tears streamed down Heather's face, "Oh Henry," Heather grabbed her chest, "where did you get this ring? It looks so familiar." Henry looked at Sadie and she smiled. "Mom?"

"Your father gave me that ring when we got married. After your father passed, I took it off and put it in that ring box - it was just too many memories. Now, hopefully it will be a part of some good new memories."

"How did you two..." Heather started.

"Sadie and I talked at the bake sale. I told her I wanted to marry you. Before I bought you a ring, she told me she had this ring. She thought it would be special for you to have," Henry said.

"Your father was a great man and I see the greatness in Henry," Sadie said, "so are you going to answer the man or not?"

Heather cried and looked Henry in the eyes, "Yes, I will marry you," she said and everyone clapped and cheered. Henry placed the ring on Heather's finger and they kissed.

"Church we are gathered here today for this is the day the Lord has made. We must rejoice and be glad in it. For God called us to come together in unity, not divided, but together praising God in love for him and for one another. Loving our neighbors as Christ loved us," the pastor opened the church service. Ms. Green, Claudia and the rest of the children's choir were in the back getting ready.

"Alright children, let's make sure your clothes are straight. Get in line now. It's almost time to go out."

Claudia was standing in the front. She tugged on Ms. Green's skirt.

"Yes angel."

"I'm glad we got to know each other Ms. Green," Claudia said.

Ms. Green started to tear up, "I'm glad too…because of you, little angel I can do what I love again…to inspire the youth to inspire the world by singing to the glory of God."

"Thank you, Ms. Green."

They listened to the preacher as he continued, "We all we got people. Let's rise together and make a difference in our community for our fellow citizens. it's time to make a difference," he said to the congregation. Henry held Heather's hand as they listened, looking at each other and smiling. Sadie said *amen* along with the congregation as the preacher talked.

"Now family, it's time to see what making a difference looks like. Let's stand to our feet and welcome our children's choir," he said as the children's choir came in. Lizzy and Jack clapped and waved at Claudia.

"Before, they sing I want to acknowledge the woman behind the choir. She has been a member here since the church doors first opened. I'm glad this opportunity came again for her to serve our youth. She is an inspirational leader and a vocalist...brothers and sisters, let's praise the Lord for Sister Priscillia Green."

Ms. Green smiled and took the microphone the pastor offered. "Thank you, pastor. Thank you everyone. Well, many of you know I used to direct the children's choir years ago. But I stopped because I lost one of our children." She paused, trying to hold back tears. Heather wiped her eyes as Ms. Green continued. "I had given up on myself. And yes family, I became cold around the church, but how many of you know God is able," she paused to a round of amens.

"One thing God won't do is fail. I was able to stay strong and I had to work on maintain my faith knowing one day Go was going to bring my life back to completion. Not too long ago I met a young lady that attends this church. A God sent child who inspired me and warmed my heart. She pushed me back to helping the youth and children ministry again. I know that her parents are very proud of her, because I know that I am," Ms. Green smiled at Claudia's parents.

"She's going to sing, Never Lost a Battle. How many of you know that God is victorious and he has never and will never lose a battle? I pray this song touches your hearts and spirits. Thank you and God bless you."

Ms. Green looked at the organist who started to play and she handed Claudia the microphone. "You better sing girl," Ms. Green winked at Claudia.

Claudia winked back and looked at the congregation, "Before we sing, I wanted to say I love God, my parents, Mrs. Cartwright and the whole church family."

"We love you too," the congregation said back to her.

The organist began to play again and Ms. Green signaled Claudia to start singing. Her voice echoed throughout the church. Lizzy held tightly to Jack's hand with tears streaming down her face. When the song ended, the congregation stood and applauded the choir. Claudia made eye contact with Heather who gave her a thumbs up.

AUTHOR'S MESSAGE

While the bake sale didn't bring in enough money for the family trip, Jack took Lizzy and Claudia for a weekend getaway. Heather continued to be a part of Claudia's life, spending time with her and being inspired by her spirit of helping others. Heather and Henry got married and Claudia was in the wedding. Sadie continued to visit Heather and Henry frequently and guiding them with her wisdom.

Heather finally understood the concept of why Claudia was brought into her life. Even though she lost her husband and child, God did not forget about her. Claudia brought life and what she saw in Claudia was the same thing in her daughter - a beautiful soul from God himself. Because of their relationship she was able to have a child like her own. God restored her loss and she was able to open her heart to love and marry Henry. God used Claudia to help bring Heather back to him.

When God wants you, he will use anything or anybody to get the message to you. Sometimes we want to give up on our faith when we go through hard and difficult times but we have to continue to trust God in the process. It may be difficult but we must remain strong in the faith. He knows what we go through. God said, "I will never leave you or forsake you." And that my friends, is enough to trust him with our lives.

www.ingramcontent.com/pod-product-compliance
Lightning Source LLC
Chambersburg PA
CBHW051450290426
44109CB00016B/1699